UNWRITTEN

The Vision Graveyard

VANCE K. JACKSON, JR.

Unwritten: The Vision Graveyard
A 21-Day Purpose Devotional
ISBN: 978-1-7369832-9-4
Published by 5th Gen Publishing, LLC.
© 2021 Vance K. Jackson, Jr.
www.VanceKJackson.com

Printed in the United States of America. All rights reserved. No portion of this book may be reproduced, stored in a retrieval system, or transmitted in any form or by any means—electronic, mechanical, photocopy, recording, scanning, or other—except for brief quotations in critical reviews or articles, without the prior written permission of the publisher.

Scripture quotations taken from the Amplified® Bible (AMPC), Copyright © 1954, 1958, 1962, 1964, 1965, 1987 by The Lockman Foundation Used by permission. www.lockman.org

Scripture quotations from The Authorized King James Version (KJV). Rights in the Authorized Version in the United Kingdom are vested in the Crown. Reproduced by permission of the Crown's patentee, Cambridge University Press.

Scripture quotations marked (MSG) are taken from THE MESSAGE, copyright © 1993, 2002, 2018 by Eugene H. Peterson. Used by permission of NavPress, represented by Tyndale House Publishers. All rights reserved.

Scripture quotations marked (NIV) are taken from the Holy Bible, New International Version®, NIV®. Copyright © 1973, 1978, 1984, 2011 by Biblica, Inc.™ Used by permission of Zondervan. All rights reserved worldwide. www.zondervan.com The "NIV" and "New International Version" are trademarks registered in the United States Patent and Trademark Office by Biblica, Inc.™

Scripture quotations marked (NLT) are taken from the Holy Bible, New Living Translation, copyright © 1996, 2004, 2015 by Tyndale House Foundation. Used by permission of Tyndale House Publishers, Inc., Carol Stream, Illinois 60188. All rights reserved.

Library of Congress Cataloging-in-Publication Data
Library of Congress Control Number: 2021912975

TABLE OF CONTENTS

DAY 1
The Vision Graveyard 9

DAY 2
The Hand of the Lord 15

DAY 3
Dry Bones Live 19

DAY 4
Can These Bones Live? 25

DAY 5
Hear Ye The Word of The Lord 29

DAY 6
And The Bones Came Together 33

DAY 7
No Breath In Them 37

DAY 8
Breathe Upon These Slain 41

DAY 9
Fear Kills Dreams 45

DAY 10
The Nations Are Waiting 49

DAY 11
Hopelessness Dries Up Destiny 53

DAY 12
I Will Open Your Graves 57

DAY 13
Let The Dead Bury The Dead .61

DAY 14
Where There Is No Vision 65

DAY 15
Man Shall Not Live By Bread Alone 69

DAY 16
Satan Desires To Sift You As Wheat. 73

DAY 17
Obedience Breaks Cycles 77

DAY 18
For I Know The Thoughts 81

DAY 19
It's Time To Launch 85

DAY 20
Toiled All Night 89

DAY 21
Be Strong And Courageous. 93

Day 1

THE VISION GRAVEYARD

The hand of the Lord was upon me, and carried me out in the spirit of the Lord, and set me down in the midst of the valley which was full of bones

EZEKIEL 37:1 KJV

Your gifts weren't meant to stay hidden. The gifts, talents, and abilities that God has given you were meant to be shared with the world. What revelation, information, and insight has God given you to feed the nations? What witty ideas, inventions, and platforms has God given you to influence and to transform generations?

What assignment has God given you to implement and to carry out? What business has God given you to build? What idea(s) has God given you to execute upon? What dream has God placed inside of your heart? You were crafted by God to lead and to transform this generation. You were born to lead. You were called to innovate.

Your gifts, talents, and abilities weren't meant to remain hidden. Your gifts were not meant to stay stagnant and dormant. Your talent wasn't meant to be marginalized. Your destiny wasn't meant to stay stuck in the valley.

The seed that God has planted inside of you wasn't meant to stay buried. You were called to steward and to nourish the seed that God has planted inside of you. What has God placed on the inside of you that was meant to be shared with the world? The world is waiting. The nations are waiting to see what God has deposited inside of you. The nations are hungry for what's inside of you. The nations are waiting to hear of the unconventional wisdom that God has deposited inside of your heart.

Proverbs 18:20 KJV declares, "A man's belly shall be satisfied with the fruit of his mouth; and with the increase of his lips shall he be filled." The world is waiting to see and to hear what's in your belly. It's time to release the wisdom that's within you. It's time to release what God has planted inside of you. It's time to release the wisdom-filled strategies that God has given you. The world needs what's inside of you.

The books, businesses, strategies, manuscripts, songs, movies, ministries, inventions, solutions, and playwrights that God has placed inside of you were meant to be shared with the world. You were called to feed the nations by releasing what God has placed inside of you. Let God unveil your gifts to the world. You are a gift to the world.

The Earth is groaning for what's inside of you. The world is yearning for the wisdom that God has placed inside of you. The nations are waiting for you to unveil what God has invested in you. The world is waiting on your obedience. The world is waiting on you to take the next step.

The world is waiting on you to deploy your God-breathed witty ideas and inventions. You were called to lead. You were called to innovate. You were called to function in your purpose. You were created to thrive. You were crafted by the Hand of God to flourish.

What witty ideas have you not yet released? What God-given ideas has God placed inside of you that you have not executed upon? What businesses are stored inside of you that you have not yet launched? What books have you not yet written? What dreams have you not yet executed upon?

Your gifts weren't meant to stay stuck in seed form. 2 Corinthians 9:10 declares, God gives seed to the sower. The New Living Translation expounds on 2 Corinthians 9:10 NLT in the following manner, "For God is the one who provides seed for the farmer and then bread to eat. In the same way, he will provide and increase your resources and then produce a great harvest of generosity in you."

Sow your gifts into others. Sow into the hearts of others. Sow into the "heart soil" of families. Choose to sow into the fabric of communities. Choose to sow into the heart of generations. What gift has God given you to sow? Who has God assigned to you to sow into? God gives wisdom to those who sow. Choose to sow.

The wisdom that God has placed inside of you, was meant to feed generations. The wisdom, information, and revelation that God has placed on the inside of you, was meant to unlock the destiny of generations. Your obedience unlocks the faith of those who are stagnant.

Your obedience serves as a clarion call to those who are wrestling with fulfilling their purpose. Your obedience, and diligent execution, is a clarion call to those whose hearts are held hostage by the grip of the enemy. Choose to obey God and execute. Choose to unleash what's inside of you.

What's inside of you could be the solution to free those who are stuck. The gifts that God has placed inside of you were meant to minister hope to the hopeless. You were created to set the captives free. Your faith, execution, and obedience will feed the faith of nations.

What gifts, talents, abilities, businesses, and ministries have God placed inside of you that you have not yet released to the world? What political office have you not yet run for? What policies have you not yet written? What boardrooms have you not yet sat in? What platform(s) is God trying to birth through you?

On the other side of your obedience, enlargement is waiting. On the other side of your execution, freedom is waiting. On the other side of your diligence, harvest is waiting. There are nations waiting on you to obey God's Word. There are generations waiting on you to obey God's Voice. There are families waiting on you to obey God's Command. There are people that's waiting for you to obey God. Release what's in your heart. Release what's in your hand. Choose to obey God and let God breathe upon the work of your hands.

Let God breathe upon everything that your hands touch. Write what God has told you to write. Build what God has told you to build. Do what God has told you to do. The Hand of the Lord is upon you.

Let God breathe upon your thoughts. Let God breathe upon your ideas. Let God breathe upon your businesses. Let God breathe upon your books, dreams, ideas, inventions, manuscripts, and playwrights. Let God breathe a fresh wind upon the work of your hands.

PRAYER

Father God, in the Name of Jesus, I thank You for leading my footsteps. Father, I thank You for guiding my path. Father God, in the Name of Jesus, let Your Hand be with me in everything that I do. Father, let Your Hand be with me in every area of my life.

Father, I thank You for every gift, every talent, and every ability that You've given me. Lord, I thank You for shaping the framework of my heart and crafting the footsteps of my destiny.

Lord, I thank You for ordering my steps. Father, I thank You for lighting my path. Father, lead me and write upon the pages of my heart. Lord, settle my heart and still every area of my life. Father, lead and direct my thoughts.

Father, let my heart reflect Your Heart. Father, I surrender to You. Lord, I surrender my gifts, talents, and abilities over to You. Father, I lay every gift, talent, and ability at Your feet. Father, I cast my crown and bow before You now and forever.

In Jesus' Name. Amen.

Day 2

THE HAND OF THE LORD

The hand of the Lord was upon me, and carried me out in the spirit of the Lord, and set me down in the midst of the valley which was full of bones

EZEKIEL 37:1 KJV

When the Hand of the Lord is upon you, you're able to do more, you're able to handle more, and your capacity increases. Proverbs 10:22 KJV declares, "The blessing of the Lord, it maketh rich, and he addeth no sorrow with it." When the Hand of the Lord is upon you, your season of toiling ends.

When the Hand of the Lord is upon you, wisdom flows easily. When the Hand of the Lord is upon you, witty ideas, inventions, and strategies are frequent and are commonplace. When the Hand of the Lord is upon you, you're able to build quicker, execute faster, and launch easier. What previously took you years to complete will take you months and days.

When the Hand of the Lord is upon you, what took others decades and generations to complete, you'll complete in mere moments. This is your moment. Now is the time. Let God order your steps. Let God lead you in the right direction. When the Hand of the Lord is upon you, your house will not shipwreck. When the Hand of the Lord is upon you, your house will not fall.

When the Hand of the Lord is upon you, God will not leave you stuck in the valley. When the Hand of the Lord is upon you, God will not leave you dying in the desert. When the Hand of the Lord is upon you, God will not let your destiny and your assignment wither. Your gifts weren't meant to stay hidden.

Your talents weren't meant to rot in the wilderness. Your destiny wasn't meant to dry up in the desert. Your gifts weren't meant to stay stagnant in the valley. Let God lead you out of the valley. Let God guide you. Let God restore you. Let God refresh you. Let God rewrite your story.

According to Ezekiel 37:1 KJV, the Hand of the Lord "carried" Ezekiel and "set him down" in the midst of a valley that was full of dry bones. Notice God's strategic placement of Ezekiel outlined in Ezekiel 37:1 KJV, "The hand of the Lord was upon me, and carried me out in the spirit of the Lord, and set me down in the midst of the valley..." God placed Ezekiel in the midst of the valley.

Take note and pay close attention to God's strategic "valley placement" of Ezekiel. Why would God place Ezekiel in the middle of a valley that was full of very dry bones? God could have placed Ezekiel anywhere within the valley in order to prove His point. God could have placed Ezekiel on the top of a mountaintop and caused Ezekiel to look down at the valley. God could have positioned Ezekiel anywhere outside of the valley. Instead, God chose to place Ezekiel right in the midst of the valley. God chose to place Ezekiel right in the midst of a seemingly dismal and dire situation. Ezekiel was surrounded by death and dry bones.

The outlook of the valley was indeed gory. Imagine being surrounded by dry bones which represents the presence of death and defeat. Imagine being surrounded by the hopelessness of this "Vision Graveyard."

Here's the point, God used Ezekiel's placement to show that He can pull anyone out of any circumstance—even if they're in the middle of a dead and dry valley. God can transform any environment. God can revive any dead circumstance. God can resurrect any dead dream. God's Word can reconstruct any abandoned vision. No matter the circumstance, no matter the situation, no matter the season, no matter the outlook—God can restore you, revive, and refresh you.

May the Hand of God lead you into your next level. May God's Hand thrust you into your next season. May the Hand of the Lord lead you to where He wants to use you next. Like Ezekiel, may God use you to transform environments. May God use your gifts, skills, talents, and abilities for His Glory. May God use you to speak life into others. May God use you to speak life into dead dreams, dry bones, and stagnant valleys.

May God use the gifts, talents, skills, and abilities that He's placed inside of you to speak life into dead dreams. May God use you to speak into the destiny of those who are stuck in the valley. May the Hand of the Lord lead you out of the valley and into your next level of success.

PRAYER

Father God, in the Name of Jesus, carry me through the valley. Father, carry me through every season of life. Father, lead me through the valley. Lord, lead me through the wilderness. Father God, in the Name of Jesus, give me the strength to go through the valley.

Father, I will not be distracted by the "dryness" of the valley. Father, I will not be distracted by the dry bones that plague the valley. Lord, lead my heart. Father, lead my mind. Father, guide my spirit. Lord, let Your Hand be with me.

Father, You can resurrect any dead dream. Father, You can restore any dead thing. Father, You can heal any old wound and fill any void. Lord, there is nothing that can compare to You. Father, Your Love is greater than the valley that I face.

Father, there is nothing that can compete with You and no one can take Your place. For You are my Lord and I completely surrender to You.

Lord, I will not be distracted by the valley that's filled with dry bones. Father, I will not be discouraged by the wilderness that surrounds me. Lord, lead my heart and guide my footsteps. Father, write upon the framework of my heart for my heart belongs to You.

In Jesus' Name. Amen.

Day 3

DRY BONES LIVE

And caused me to pass by them round about: and, behold, there were very many in the open valley; and, lo, they were very dry.

EZEKIEL 37:2 KJV

In addition to God placing Ezekiel in the midst of the valley—God caused Ezekiel to also "pass by" these very dry bones. The New Living Translation expounds on Ezekiel 37:2 NLT in the following manner, "He led me all around among the bones..." Notice, The New Living Translation highlights the fact that God set Ezekiel in the middle of the valley and then he led him around these very dry bones.

Look at this important moment, nestled within this verse, God led Ezekiel *past* these dry bones. God led Ezekiel past those who were dead. God led Ezekiel past the dead circumstance of others. God caused Ezekiel to pass by the dead and stagnant things that riddled the valley.

Choose to remember this principle whenever you're facing a dry season or a valley. Remember that God will always lead you through the valley and past the dead circumstance of others. Let God lead you past the stagnation of others.

Choose to remember that the valley is temporary. Choose not to focus on the stagnation of those that lay in the valley. Choose not to focus on those whose hearts are spiritually stuck and emotionally drained in the valley. Choose to focus on God. Choose to focus forward. Choose to focus on the future.

Although Ezekiel was surrounded by the dead things of the valley—notice that Ezekiel did not allow the stagnation of the valley to stunt his purpose, assignment, and his perspective. Even when Ezekiel was in the valley he chose to trust God.

Notice, even when Ezekiel was in the valley, he still obeyed God's Voice. Ezekiel didn't allow the death that plagued the valley to distract him from obeying God's Voice. Ezekiel did not allow the dead circumstance of those that surrounded him to discourage him from moving forward in his destiny.

Don't let the death of the valley cause you to stop moving forward in your purpose. God's Authority overrules the death and stagnation of the valley. Go through the valley and do what God has called you to do. Just because the insight, innovation, witty ideas, and inventions have dried up and withered in others that surround you—choose to move forward in your purpose.

There is life in you. God will not cause your story to be left unwritten. Let God write your story. God's Hand is on you to do more. God's Hand is on you to be more. God's Hand is on you to see more. Let God use you beyond the devastation of the valley. God has given you victory over the valley.

Let God use you to speak to the "dryness" of the valley. Let God use you to transform the story of those stuck in the valley. You weren't born to die in the valley. You were created to give God glory. Let His light shine through you. Let His light shine through the work of your hands.

The mandate that's on your life is not determined by the stagnation of the valley. When the Hand of the Lord is upon you, the dryness of the valley has no authority over you. Don't let the impotency of others stop you from being fruitful. Speak life into the valley. Don't let the valley discourage you. Don't let the valley distract you. Don't let the valley derail you.

Take note of what Ezekiel 37:2 KJV declares, "Ezekiel passed by 'very dry' bones." The Bible also highlights that these bones were "very dry." These bones were not only dead and dry—they were "very dry" which signifies that the moment of death and the process of deterioration had completed a long time ago. In other words, there was absolutely no sign of life in the valley. In fact, the flesh on these very dry bones had completely dried up.

The muscles and ligaments that were attached to these very dry bones had deteriorated, separated, and decayed a long time ago. In other words, this valley was not only full of dry bones it was also full of dead vision, unfulfilled dreams, underutilized gifts, talents, skills, and abilities. As we will soon see, those who died here in the valley were filled with hopelessness. Those who died here were stuck and had no vision for the future. Don't let your destiny die in the valley. Don't let your outlook on the future grow dim.

What vision has God placed on the inside of you that's slowly dying because you've allowed "the valley" to stifle your destiny? What gift(s) have you buried because you've allowed fear to stifle your execution? What dreams have you allowed to gather dust because of slothfulness?

Let God use the gifts, talents, and abilities that He's planted on the inside of you to reach the world. Let God use the gifts, talents, and abilities that He's planted on the inside of you to feed the nations. Don't let your gifts lie dormant. Don't let your talents rot in the hopelessness of the valley. Don't let what God has placed on the inside of you decay. It's time to execute. It's time to move forward.

James 2:26 KJV declares, "For as the body without the spirit is dead, so faith without works is dead also." Faith without work is dead. The world is waiting for you to work your gift. The world is waiting to hear what you have to say. The world is waiting to see what's in your hands.

What wisdom has God placed inside of you that He wants you to reveal to the world? The world is waiting to see what your hands will produce. The world is waiting to read what your fingers will write. The world is waiting to see what your hands will build. The world is waiting on you to execute.

Make a move and do what you've been called to do. Don't let your gifts die in the valley. Pursue everything that God has called you to do. It's time to build. It's time to lead. It's time to execute. Now is the time to function in your purpose. Choose to function in your call. Dry bones hear the Word of the Lord—and live!

PRAYER

Father God, in the Name of Jesus, Lord I thank You for leading me past the "dry bones" of the valley. Father, I thank You for not allowing me to settle in the valley. Father, I thank You for not allowing me to settle in the valley of complacency and mediocrity. Father, I choose to continue to move forward in You.

Lord, every aspect of my heart surrenders to You. Lord, bless the work of my hands and breathe upon every aspect of my life. Father, I belong to You. My heart belongs to You. My gifts belong to You. My talent belongs to You. My abilities belong to You. Father, my destiny belongs to You.

Father, You are my Lord, and everything that my hands and heart produce belongs to You. Father, You are my Lord and King—and I choose to bow to You.

My lips will sing Your praise. My heart will worship You forever. Lord, I choose to honor You. Lord, I choose to lift You high above all of my fears, concerns, cares, and worries. Father, I choose to let the weight of the valley go.

Father, write upon the tablet of my heart. Father, I will not allow the cares of the valley to distract me from pursuing my purpose. Father, I will heed to Your command and follow You forever. Lord, lead and shape the framework of my heart. Father, I choose to look to You.

In Jesus' Name. Amen.

Day 4

CAN THESE BONES LIVE?

And he said unto me, Son of man, can these bones live? And I answered, O Lord God, thou knowest.

EZEKIEL 37:3 KJV

In Ezekiel 37:3 KJV, God asked Ezekiel, "Can these bones live?" In other words, God asked Ezekiel, can the dead dreams of those who've died here in the valley live again? Can the vision of those who've died here live again? Can those who have lost hope live again?

According to Strong's Concordance, the Hebrew word for, "Live", is "Chayah" (H2421) which means, "To revive, make alive, nourish up, preserve, quicken, recover, repair, restore to life, to be whole." In Ezekiel 37:3 KJV, when God asked Ezekiel, "Can these bones live?" God already knew the answer. When God asks a question—He already knows the answer. God already knew what He was about to do in the valley.

No matter the circumstance. No matter the situation. God has the authority to revive any dead dream. No matter how seemingly dead your circumstance, God has the power to reverse, revive, quicken, recover, repair, and restore any dead dream. God has the Power to restore and reverse any dead dream that has been dead for years, decades—or even for generations.

Joel 2:25-26 KJV declares, "And I will restore to you the years that the locust hath eaten, the cankerworm, and the caterpiller, and the palmerworm, my great army which I sent among you. And ye shall eat in plenty, and be satisfied, and praise the Name of the Lord your God, that hath dealt wondrously with you: and my people shall never be ashamed."

God wants to restore every aspect of your life. God wants to restore every aspect of your destiny that has been lying dormant. God wants to heal the old wounds of the past. God wants to use you in incredible and mighty ways.

God has the power to heal you. God wants to make you whole. God does not want the gifts, talents, abilities, dreams, vision, and ideas that He's placed in you—to die in the valley.

Let God revive the dream that you've abandoned. Let God restore the vision that you've let go of. Let God nourish the gifts, talents, and abilities that you've allowed to dry up.

If you've lost hope—choose to trust in the God of Hope. If you've lost your strength—choose to lean upon the God of Strength. Choose to let God be your strength and your shield. Let God restore you. Let God heal you. Let God make you whole.

PRAYER

Father God, in the Name of Jesus, my hope is in You. Father, my strength is in You. Father, I believe that dry dreams can be restored. Father, I thank You for reviving the destiny that You have set up for me.

Father, You can restore any dead and dry dream. Father, write upon the framework of my destiny. Lord, lead me. Lord, guide me. Father, death has no authority over You. Father, fear has no place in You. Lord, You are my Rock, Refuge, and Strong Tower.

Father, my heart safely trusts in You. For You are my King, my Lord, and my Savior. Father, my heart will forever surrender to You.

In Jesus' Name. Amen.

Day 5

HEAR YE THE WORD OF THE LORD

Again he said unto me, Prophesy upon these bones, and say unto them, O ye dry bones, hear the word of the Lord.

EZEKIEL 37:4 KJV

According to Strong's Concordance, the Hebrew word for, "Hear", used in Ezekiel 37:4 KJV is "Shama" (H8085) which means, "Listen to or to obey." Dry bones, hear ye the Word of the Lord. Dry dreams, listen to the Word of the Lord. Dry vision, obey ye the Word of the Lord. Old forgotten about things, hear ye the Word of the Lord. Let every part of your life hear, obey, listen to, and receive the Word of the Lord. Let His Word reign in every area of your life. Choose to obey His Word. Choose to obey His Promises and His Way of doing things.

Ezekiel 37:5 KJV declares, "Thus saith the Lord God unto these bones; Behold, I will cause breath to enter into you, and ye shall live:" God will cause His breath to breathe into your circumstance. God will cause His breath to infiltrate your dead dreams.

God will cause His breath to breathe life into your dead vision—if you let Him. Let God breathe into your dead dreams. Let God breathe into your life. Let God breathe into your vision. Let God breathe into your future.

According to Strong's Concordance, the Hebrew word for, "Breath", used in Ezekiel 37:5 KJV, is "Ruwach" (H7307) which means, "Spirit of God, wind of heaven". In other words—let the breath of God breathe life into your circumstance. Let His wind breathe life into the heart of the matter.

There is no dead thing that God cannot resurrect. His Power is stronger than the dead circumstance that you face. The breath of God, or the *Ruwach* of God, is stronger than the death of the valley. The *Ruwach* of God is stronger than the stench of the hopeless circumstance. The breath of God will breathe new life into any dead and dry valley.

God wants to breathe His breath into your life. Do not worry about the bones that surround you. Don't worry about the death of the valley. The valley does not determine the direction of your destiny.

God holds your destiny in His Hands. He is the Author and Finisher of your destiny. The hopelessness of those that surround you does not dictate your purpose. The dry bones that surround you do not determine who God has called you to be.

Let the *Ruwach* of God breathe into your nostrils and put the pieces back together. When God breathes His breath on your circumstance there is nothing that can stop His Power from moving on your behalf.

Notice what Ezekiel 37:6 KJV declares, "And I will lay sinews upon you, and will bring up flesh upon you, and cover you with skin, and put breath in you, and ye shall live; and ye shall know that I am the Lord."

The New International Version expounds on Ezekiel 37:6 NIV in the following manner, "I will attach tendons to you and make flesh come upon you and cover you with skin; I will put breath in you, and you will come to life. Then you will know that I am the Lord."

Not only will God breathe upon the "bone" of a matter, He will breathe upon the "core" of a thing. God will also cause the "tendons" of the vision to come together. In other words, God will connect the proper pieces together, and God will cause the intricate details to come together—at the appropriate time.

When you trust God's Way of doing things, He can orchestrate things and set things in order in His season. Trust His timing. Trust His plan. Trust in Christ. His Way is better. Dry bones hear ye the Word of the Lord and live!

PRAYER

Father God, in the Name of Jesus, my heart trusts in You. Father, there is hope in You. Father, there is life in You. Father, there is healing in You. Father, there is joy in You. Father, there is strength in You.

Father, I decree that every area of my life will hear, obey, and heed to Your Voice. Father, let every area of my life reflect Your Word. Father, You rule, reign, and have dominion over every area of my life.

Father, I choose to obey Your Way. Father, I choose to grab hold of Your Promises. I choose to do things Your Way. Father, I choose to trust in Your timing.

Breathe upon my life. Breathe upon my circumstance. Breathe upon every area of my life. Breathe upon my thoughts. Breathe upon my ideas. Breathe upon my mind. Breathe upon every area of my life.

In Jesus' Name. Amen.

Day 6

AND THE BONES CAME TOGETHER

So I prophesied as I was commanded: and as I prophesied, there was a noise, and behold a shaking, and the bones came together, bone to his bone.

EZEKIEL 37:7 KJV

Don't worry—the vision is coming together. Believe God—the dream is coming together. Stay focused—the idea is coming together. The bones are coming together. The blueprint is coming together. The pieces are coming together. Trust God—it's all coming together.

Notice, before Ezekiel spoke in Ezekiel 37:7 KJV, that the bones in the valley were scattered all across the floor of the valley. Think about it, these bones were not only very dry, but they were also laid out across the valley in a disorganized and dismembered fashion.

Think about this picture for a moment. When something dies in the wilderness, the process of death is indeed gory. After the moment of death, the flesh from each bone begins to deteriorate.

Soon thereafter, the flesh from each bone begins to separate from the skeletal frame and is picked apart and devoured by the scavenging birds of the air and the beasts of the valley. Needless to say, the very dry bones that Ezekiel saw in the valley were far past the point of death. There was indeed no hope or life found in them.

Here's the point, it doesn't matter what enemy has devoured your dreams. God has the final say. God's Authority outranks the beasts of the valley. God's Authority overrules the process of death and defeat. God has the Power to bring the pieces together.

It doesn't matter what ravenous beast of the field has picked apart your dreams—God has the Power to connect you with the right people. God has the Power to put you in the right place. He has the Power to put you in the proper position at the appropriate time. He holds time in His Hands. He holds opportunity in His Hands.

It doesn't matter who has tried to eat up your flesh. It doesn't matter what beasts of the valley have tried to devour your hopes and dreams—God's Authority overrules the deterioration of the valley. God's Word is stronger than the valley that you face.

Psalms 27:2 KJV declares, "When the wicked, even mine enemies and my foes, came upon me to eat up my flesh, they stumbled and fell." The New International Version expounds on Psalms 27:2 NIV in the following manner, "When the wicked advance against me to devour me, it is my enemies and my foes who will stumble and fall." May your enemies stumble and fall.

PRAYER

Father God, in the Name of Jesus, You are greater than the valley that I face. Father, You are greater than the storm that comes my way. Father, You are stronger than the wind and waves that try to sink my ship. Father, You are my fortress and my guide.

Father, You are greater than the wild beasts of the valley. Father, You are greater than the enemies that I face. Father, I choose to exalt You. I choose to worship and honor You. Lord, I choose to magnify You.

Father, Your Way is better. Your Way is more excellent. Father, Your Way is more powerful, and I choose to trust You. Father, You are my Potter, and I am your clay.

Father, I believe that the pieces are coming together. Father, I believe that the vision is coming together. Father, I believe that the dream is coming together and I choose to trust in You more than the dream. Father, I choose to trust in You more than the promise.

In Jesus' Name. Amen.

Day 7

NO BREATH IN THEM

Then as I watched, muscles and flesh formed over the bones. Then skin formed to cover their bodies, but they still had no breath in them.

EZEKIEL 37:8 NLT

Imagine the number of dreams that died in this valley. Imagine the number of people who died in this very valley with vision still left in them. Imagine the number of people who didn't complete what God had assigned them to accomplish who lie here in this valley.

Imagine the number of people who were holding on to partially written books. Imagine the number of partially executed dreams. Imagine the number of half-baked ideas. Imagine the number of businesses, inventions, and innovations that lay here in this valley that was full of dry bones.

Don't be like those stuck in the valley—obey God and watch God resurrect old dreams. Choose to obey God and watch God breathe new life into you. Choose to obey God and watch God move.

Despite the devastation that surrounded Ezekiel, take note of this very important principle found in Ezekiel 37:8, Ezekiel chose to obey God and he declared the Word of the Lord. No matter the situation, no matter the circumstance—choose to declare the Word of the Lord.

Ezekiel obeyed God, and then he watched the flesh and skin form around the very dry bones. Choose to obey God and then watch God move on your behalf.

The Amplified Version expounds on Ezekiel 37:8 AMPC in the following manner, "And I looked and behold, there were sinews upon [the bones] and flesh came upon them and skin covered them over, but there was no breath or spirit in them."

Notice the last part of Ezekiel 37:8 AMPC, "But there was no breath or spirit in them." Something was missing. The bones were standing up—but something was missing. The skeletal infrastructure was in place—but something was still missing. The vision had flesh and muscles—but there was something still missing. In other words, the vision "looked" the part—but something was missing.

You may have built the vision—but there's something still missing. You may have built the business—but there's no life in it. You may have obeyed God and written that book—but there's still something missing. Let God bring the pieces together. Let God breathe into the vision.

Let God breathe life into what He told you to write. Let God breathe life into what He told you to build. Let God breathe life into what He's told you to do. What has God told you to build? What has God told you to do? What assignment has God given you to accomplish?

What talent has God given you to share with the world? What gift, skill, or ability has God placed inside of you to feed the world? It's your choice to either feed the world or to feed the valley. Feed the world or choose to stay stagnant.

Don't die with unused gifts, talents, and abilities buried inside of you. Your gifts weren't meant to rot in the valley. Don't let your talents stay stagnant in the desert. You have the choice—exercise your faith and put your gifts to work or let fear keep you stuck in the wilderness. You choose. Don't let fear paralyze your destiny.

PRAYER

Father God, in the Name of Jesus, I surrender my gifts, talents, and abilities over to You. Father, I choose to lay them at Your feet. Father, I choose to worship You and not the gifts that You've given me.

Father, You are greater than the gifts that You've given me. Father, I choose to use my gifts, skills, talents, and abilities to advance Your Kingdom. Lord, I choose not to waste the gifts that You've poured into me.

Father, I choose not to bury the talents that You've invested in me. Lord, I will not let the talents that You've poured into me die in the wilderness. Father, I refuse to let the gifts that You have given me rot in the valley.

Father God, in the Name of Jesus, I will steward the opportunities that You've given me well. Lord, I will shepherd the gifts that You've given me well. Father, I will manage and oversee the resources that You've given me and steward them well.

Father, I will steward and multiply the talents that You've poured into me. Father, I refuse to let the gifts, skills, and talents that You've given me lie waste in the wilderness. Fear will not hold me back from pursuing everything that You have prepared for me.

In Jesus' Name. Amen.

Day 8

BREATHE UPON THESE SLAIN

Then said he unto me, Prophesy unto the wind, prophesy, son of man, and say to the wind, Thus saith the Lord God; Come from the four winds, O breath, and breathe upon these slain, that they may live.

EZEKIEL 37:9 KJV

When God speaks, dead dreams come alive. There is nothing that can overrule God's Word. There's nothing that can overrule God's Command. When God Commands your dreams to live, no one can stop your success.

"Then he said to me, "Speak a prophetic message to the winds, son of man. Speak a prophetic message and say, 'This is what the Sovereign Lord says: Come, O breath, from the four winds! Breathe into these dead bodies so they may live again.'" Ezekiel 37:9 NLT. Let God breathe upon your thoughts. Let God breathe upon your ideas. Let God breathe upon your dreams.

Let the breath of God breathe upon every aspect of your life. Let the breath of God rest upon every part of your heart. Let His Word supernaturally break every yoke. Let His Word break every bondage. Let His Word break every cycle. Let His Word break every generational yoke.

Let the breath of God breathe upon everything that your hands touch. Let the breath of God breathe upon your thoughts. Let the breath of God breathe upon your unfinished projects. Let God breathe upon the assignments that He has given you to complete. Let God breathe upon the work that He's ordered you to finish. Finish the work. Finish the assignment. God has given you the Grace to finish.

God wants to breathe into your unfinished assignments. Pick up that unfinished degree. Pick up that unfinished book. Finish writing that song. Publish that manuscript. Deploy that movie. Finish building that building. Launch that business. Complete that dream. Finish your assignment. Let God breathe life into you again.

PRAYER

Father God, in the Name of Jesus, breathe upon the works of my hands. Father God, breathe upon the framework of my heart. Father, breathe upon my ideas.

Lord, grant me the wisdom to try again. Father, give me the strength to build again. Father, grant me the grace to lead again. Father, I am Your servant. Lord, lead my path. Father, guide my footsteps. Father, guide the inner workings of my heart.

Father, let Your Word cultivate the soil of my heart. Father, let Your Word cover me. Father, let Your Word hold me up in the middle of the storm. Father, grant me the grace to finish what You've placed in me to complete.

Father, You are my Source. You are my Strong Tower. Father, in You I am complete. Father, in You I am made whole. Father, there is no lack in You. Father, there is no fear in You. There is no failure in You. Father, let Your Word light my path. Let Your Word steer my course. Father, lead the work of my hands.

In Jesus' Name. Amen.

Day 9

FEAR KILLS DREAMS

For God has not given us a spirit of fear and timidity, but of power, love, and self-discipline.

2 TIMOTHY 1:7 NLT

Fear is a dream killer. Fear will stunt and stifle your destiny. Fear kills dreams that never had a chance to form. Fear kills dreams that never had a chance to grow. Fear kills dreams that never had a chance to blossom. Fear kills dreams while they're still in "seed form". Fear kills dreams while they're still in the womb.

Fear will paralyze your purpose. Fear wants to devour and dismantle your destiny. Fear wants to paralyze your gifts. Fear wants to silence your dreams.

When fear speaks louder than your faith, your gifts begin to wither. When fear speaks louder than the Word of God, your gifts begin to shrivel. God does not want you to shrink back in fear.

God did not give you the spirit of fear. God gave you gifts, talents, skills, and abilities in order to glorify Him. God did not give you witty ideas, inventions, and strategies in order for them to lie dormant in the valley.

Give birth to those businesses. Launch that ministry. Finish that book. Release what God has planted in you. The world is waiting. Fear will choke your dreams and kill your harvest. Fear will keep your household in bondage.

Fear will stagnate the destiny of generations. Release what God has placed inside of you. Don't allow fear to lord over your dreams. Don't allow fear to lord over your destiny.

God wants to breathe life into you again. God wants to breathe into your dreams again. God wants to breathe into your gifts, talents, and abilities again. God wants to give you a fresh start.

God wants you to hope again. He wants you to live again. God wants to breathe into every aspect of your life. God wants to revive the things that you have let go of. That dead dream that's been lying dormant—let God breathe life into it again.

Ezekiel 37:9 NLT declares, "Then he said to me, Speak a prophetic message to the winds, son of man. Speak a prophetic message and say, 'This is what the Sovereign Lord says: Come, O breath, from the four winds! Breathe into these dead bodies so they may live again.'"

You cannot do "it" without the breath of God. You can't build without the breath of God. You can't lead without the Hand of God. You can't execute without the breath of God.

Let the breath of God breathe upon the work of your hands. Let God breathe into your dead dreams. Let God breathe upon the work and fruit of your hands. Choose to divorce the stronghold of fear and marry yourself to God's Word.

PRAYER

Father God, in the Name of Jesus, I repent for letting fear lord over my actions. Father, I choose to bow to You, and I break the cycle of fear from operating in my life.

Father, I choose to move forward in You. Father, I choose to take the next step forward in You. Father, You are my Shepherd. Father, You are my Guide. You are my Provider, and I shall lack nothing.

Father God, in the Name of Jesus, I rebuke the spirit of fear from operating in my bloodline. Fear has no place in my life. Fear has no place in my destiny. Fear has no authority in my life. Fear will not rule over any area of my heart.

Father, I surrender to You. Father, let Your Peace rule and rest in every area of my heart. Father, let Your Presence rest and dwell in every area of my life.

In Jesus' Name. Amen.

Day 10

THE NATIONS ARE WAITING

So I prophesied as he commanded me, and the breath came into them, and they lived, and stood up upon their feet, an exceeding great army.

EZEKIEL 37:10 KJV

According to Ezekiel 37:10 KJV, notice what happens when God breathes His breath into these dry bones, "So I prophesied as he commanded me, and the breath came into them, and they lived, and stood up upon their feet..."

When God breathes life into your vision—it stands up. You can have the framework, the blueprint, the resources, and all of the seemingly right pieces together—but without the breath of God, you'll have built a framework without life.

Let God breathe into your dreams, plans, and vision. Let God breathe into the framework of your life. Let God breathe into your dreams. Let God breathe into your family. Let God breathe into your womb. Let God breathe into your heart. Let God breathe into your thoughts, ideas, plans, and dreams.

Only God can bring the dream to life. Only God can transform the old and make it new. Only God can restore what was once dead and lost. May God breathe upon the work of your hands. May God breathe upon your writing. May God breathe upon your business. May God breathe upon your business plans. May God establish you. May He establish your thoughts. May He stabilize you. May He turn you into an exceedingly great army.

What God has put inside of you was not meant to stay dormant. You were meant to dominate. Your gifts were meant to feed the nations. Your gifts weren't meant to stay hidden—your gifts were meant to feed generations. The gifts, talents, ideas, skills, abilities, and innovations that are inside of you were meant to be cultivated, developed, and sharpened.

May God develop the gifts that He's placed inside of you. May God develop the talents that He's put inside of you. May God strengthen the abilities that He's invested in you. May your dreams, talents, gifts, and abilities glorify God.

May what God has placed inside of you shine and reflect the Glory of God on your job, in business, in the boardroom, in your community, within the walls of your city, in your nation, and throughout the Earth. May your light shine. May the light that God has placed inside of you Glorify the True and Living King.

May the gifts that God has placed in you magnify God. Let the talents that God has placed inside of you glorify the King. The world is waiting to hear what God has placed in your mouth.

The Earth is groaning to see what God has placed in your heart. Generations are waiting to hear what's in your belly. Let God use you. Pour out what God has poured into you. The nations are waiting.

PRAYER

Father God, in the Name of Jesus, I thank You for the gifts, talents, and abilities that You've poured into me. Father, I choose to reflect Your Heart and Character in every area of my life. Father, I surrender to You.

Father, I choose to magnify You in my job, in my business, in the boardroom, in private, and in public. Father, I surrender to You in every area of my life.

Father, it is Your breath in me that propels my destiny. Father, stabilize my heart. Father, stabilize every area of my life.

Father, let the gifts that You've placed in me glorify You. Lord, let the talents that You've placed inside of me magnify You. Father, I surrender every area of my life over to You. Father, You are my Source.

Father, You are my Strength. Father, till the ground of my heart. Father, give me the courage to pour out what You have poured in me out to the world.

In Jesus' Name. Amen.

Day 11

HOPELESSNESS DRIES UP DESTINY

Then he said unto me, Son of man, these bones are the whole house of Israel: behold, they say, Our bones are dried, and our hope is lost: we are cut off for our parts.

EZEKIEL 37:11 KJV

What has God placed inside of you that you've allowed to lie dormant? What Kingdom-minded businesses has God placed inside of you that you've allowed to let sit? What Purpose-driven initiative has God placed inside of you that you've allowed to lie stagnant and stuck?

What have you lost hope for? What dream(s) have you given up on? What plans have you lost hope for? Maybe, you're like the House of Israel described here in Ezekiel 37:11 KJV, "Our bones are dried, and our hope is lost: we are cut off for our parts." Maybe, you feel like you're "cut" off for your parts.

Maybe, you feel like you're drained of energy and you've lost hope for the future. Maybe, you're weary and you don't have the energy to try again. Maybe, you don't have the energy to build again.

Maybe, you've lost hope and you don't have the energy to write again. Maybe, you've lost hope and you don't have the energy to study again. Maybe, you've lost hope and you don't have the energy to pen another song.

Maybe, you don't have the energy to pen another policy. Maybe, you don't have the energy to pen another speech. Maybe, you've lost hope and you don't have the energy to pen another message. Choose to hope again. Choose to dream again. Choose to build again. Choose to lead again.

My child, do not give up. Do not give in. The harvest that God has prepared for you—is for you. Let God breathe into you again. Let the *Ruwach* of God give you the strength to try again. Let His Breath give you the courage to soar again. Let God give you the audacity to build again. Let God give you the faith to write again.

The words that God has penned upon the walls of your heart were meant to lead and transform the heart of generations. The wisdom, witty ideas, and inventions that God has poured into you were meant to lead and change the world. Put your hands to the plow and let God breathe into the work of your hands.

Let God raise up the work of your hands. Let God elevate the work of your heart. Let God use what's inside of you to heal families, build communities, and lead nations. Hopelessness will slowly strangle and choke the life out of your destiny. Don't let hopelessness steal what God has planted inside of you.

You have a generational mandate. You were not meant to be normal. You were not meant to be ordinary. You were not meant to stay stuck in a cycle of mediocrity. You were built to be extraordinary. You were meant to share your gifts with the world.

What's keeping you stagnant? What's preventing you from pursuing your purpose? What barriers have blocked your destiny? What mental framework has restricted you from pursuing everything that God has for you? Don't let the things of this world stop you from pursuing everything that God has called you to be.

Don't let the cares of life choke your harvest. Don't let the cares of this world suffocate your skills, talents, and abilities. Do what God has called you to do. Write what God has called you to write. Build what God has called you to build. Lead what God has called you to lead.

Hopelessness will cause your dreams to stay stuck in seed form. Don't shrink. Choose to let hopelessness die and grab a hold onto the Promises of God. Do what God is calling you to do and come out of the graveyard of hopelessness. It's time to pursue. It's time to run. It's time to lead and build everything that God has for you.

PRAYER

Father God, in the Name of Jesus, You are my Hope and Strength. Father, let Your Wisdom flow through me. Father, use my hands to build Your Kingdom.

Father, I surrender every witty idea, innovation, and invention over to You. Father, I choose to put my hands to the plow. Father, let Your Breath breathe life into the work of my hands.

Father, cover me. Lord, lead me. Father, let the work of my hands honor you and bless the nations. Father, I refuse to let fear rob me of not fulfilling the destiny that You have designed for me.

Father, I refuse to stay stuck in a cycle of stagnation. Lord, let Your Light shine through me.

In Jesus' Name. Amen.

Day 12

I WILL OPEN YOUR GRAVES

> *Therefore prophesy and say unto them, Thus saith the Lord God; Behold, O my people, I will open your graves, and cause you to come up out of your graves, and bring you into the land of Israel.*
>
> EZEKIEL 37:12 KJV

Let God open up the graves of your heart. Let His Word heal and restore areas that you didn't think needed to be touched. Don't let hopelessness rob you of your execution. Let the rejection of the past go. Let the bitterness of "the last" go. Let your past failures go. Let your past failed attempts go. Don't let the weight of the past weigh you down.

Let the shortcomings of the past go. Divorce yourself from the weight of condemnation and let the weight and burden of the past go. Let the heart entanglements of the past go. Let the weight and cares of the past go.

Don't let the past lord over your heart. Don't carry the dead weight of the past into your future. Today is a new day. Now is the season. Now is the time. God has given you a fresh start.

Let God resurrect the parts of your heart that you've allowed to die. Leave the weight of the past in the valley of dry bones. Forgive yourself. Forgive others. Choose to be set free from the imprisonment of fear, failure, and hopelessness.

When God leads you out of bondage—choose not to return to the dead things of the past. Let God lead you into the land of Promise. Let God lead you into everything that He has for you. Your heart cannot grow if you're still holding on to the dead weight of the past. You can't innovate if you're holding on to the dead framework of the past. You can't build something new if you're still focused on the dead things of the past.

Let God do a new thing within the borders of your heart. Let God do something new within the borders of your life. God wants to do something new through the work of your hands. God wants to do something new, fresh, and innovative through you. The world is waiting to hear what you have to say. The world is waiting to see what God has imprinted on your heart. Let the past go and embrace what God has for you.

Ezekiel 37:14 KJV declares, "And shall put my spirit in you, and ye shall live, and I shall place you in your own land: then shall ye know that I the Lord have spoken it, and performed it, saith the Lord."

When you let the past go and embrace God's Way of doing things, He shall lead you to your own land. May God lead you into the land that He's prepared for you. May the Lord breathe upon your circumstance. May God breathe upon your dry bones. May God breathe upon your dry dreams. May God breathe upon your old dead vision.

May God breathe upon the work of your hands. May the Lord lead you out of the valley. May God breathe hope into you again. May the Breath of God breathe life into you again.

God is greater than your past. God is greater than the valley that you face.

PRAYER

Father God, in the Name of Jesus, breathe into the framework of my life. Father, breathe into every corner of my family. Holy Spirit, breathe into every aspect of my life, destiny, and purpose.

Father, I belong to You. Father, I choose to serve and honor You. Father, You are my Lord and I heed to Your Voice. Father, I heed to Your Command. Lord, lead me. Lord, lead the work of my hands.

Father, guide my footsteps. Father, order my steps. Lord, lead me on the path of righteousness. Father, I submit my gifts, talents, and abilities over to You. Father, there is no one like You in all the Earth.

Father, You are my *El-Shaddai*. You are God Almighty. Father, I surrender to You. Father, my heart bows to You. Lord, write Your Words upon my heart.

Lord, I choose to renounce pride. I choose to renounce rejection. In the Name of Jesus, I choose to renounce hopelessness, bitterness, and condemnation. Father, there is hope in You. Father, there is joy in You. Father, there is peace in You. Father, I am whole in You.

In Jesus' Name, I choose to let the weight of the past go. Father, I choose to let the entanglement of the past go. Father, I surrender to You—now and forever.

In Jesus' Name. Amen.

Day 13

LET THE DEAD BURY THE DEAD

Jesus said unto him, Let the dead bury their dead: but go thou and preach the kingdom of God.

LUKE 9:60 KJV

According to Strong's Concordance, the Greek word for "Dead" is, "nekros" (G3498) which means, "One that has breathed his last, lifeless, spiritually dead, destitute of a life that recognizes and is devoted to God, inactive as respects doing right, destitute of force or power, inactive, and inoperative."

In Luke 9:60 KJV, Jesus commands this man to let the dead bury the dead. Before making the decision to fully follow Christ—this man asked to go back to bury his father. This seems like a reasonable request—until Jesus gives His response. Jesus responded to this man by saying, "Let the dead bury the dead".

The Amplified Version expounds on Luke 9:60 AMPC in the following manner, "But Jesus said to him, Allow the dead to bury their own dead; but as for you, go and publish abroad throughout all regions the kingdom of God." Jesus declared to this young man, "Let the dead bury the dead. Your duty is to go and preach about the Kingdom of God to all the nations."

The New Living Translation expounds upon Luke 9:60 NLT in the following manner, "But Jesus told him, Let the spiritually dead bury their own dead! Your duty is to go and preach about the Kingdom of God." Jesus declares to the young man—to leave behind those who are spiritually dead, powerless, inactive, and inoperative—and to let the dead bury the dead.

Let the stagnant bury the stagnant. Let the fearful bury the fearful. Let the slothful bury the slothful. Let the spiritually inactive bury the spiritually inactive. But as for you—there is life in you. As for you—it's time to transform the world. As for you—it's time to go into the world and preach the gospel.

Don't let your gifts, talents, abilities, and ideas die with "dead" people. Don't let your gifts die with the inactive. Don't let your gifts die with the unbelieving. Don't let your gifts die with the doubters. Don't let your gifts be strangled by the slothful.

God wants what He's placed inside of you to flourish. Inactive people are full of sloth and will keep you inactive. Inactive people are full of vision but lack execution. Inactive people are full of ideas but lack the process to fulfill what God has told them to do. Inoperative people are full of excuses and they refuse to fully execute.

The spiritually destitute and lazy will die with unfulfilled dreams and destinies within their hearts. But as for you, Jesus declares in Luke 9:60, you will not die full. Your charge is to go to the nations and proclaim His Gospel. Proclaim God's Good News. Choose to fulfill what God has written in the walls of your heart.

Your gifts weren't meant to stay inactive. Your gifts weren't meant to stay dormant. Your gifts weren't meant to stay hidden. Your gifts were meant to light up the world. In Matthew 5:14 KJV, Jesus puts it this way, "Ye are the light of the world. A city that is set on an hill cannot be hid."

You are a "light" that's set on a hill. You are an example for the world to see. You are a "Lively Light." Your life was meant to be put on display as an example for generations to follow. Your gifts were placed inside of you for the world to follow. Let your gifts shine. Let the dead bury the dead. It's time for you to light up the world.

PRAYER

Father God, in the Name of Jesus, I choose to let the past go. Father, I choose to follow You. Lord, I choose to let the inactive habits of the past go.

Father, I choose to let the old framework of the past go. Lord, I choose to let the fruit of my lips honor You. Father, I choose to let the fruit of my heart honor You. Father, I choose to let the work of my hands and the gifts of my heart honor You. Lord, let every aspect of my life, both in private and public, honor You.

Father, I will choose to let the dead bury the dead. Lord, I will choose to serve and honor You all the days of my life. Father, I choose this day, to let my life serve as an example for generations to follow.

Father, I love You with my whole heart. Father, I honor You with my whole heart. Father, I choose to serve You. Father, with everything that's within me, let my life Praise and Glorify Your Name.

In Jesus' Name. Amen.

Day 14

WHERE THERE IS NO VISION

*Where there is no vision, the people perish:
but he that keepeth the law, happy is he.*

PROVERBS 29:18 KJV

Notice how the Amplified Version expounds upon Proverbs 29:18 AMPC, "Where there is no vision [no redemptive revelation of God], the people perish; but he who keeps the law [of God, which includes that of man]–blessed (happy, fortunate, and enviable) is he."

Your vision wasn't meant to stay hidden. Your vision wasn't meant to stay silent. Your vision wasn't meant to stay dormant. Where there is no redemptive revelation of God—the people perish. Where there is no revealed Word of God—you will perish.

The vision that's inside of you was not meant to perish. Your God-breathed vision was meant to praise and glorify God. The creative gifts that are inside of you were meant to reveal and reflect the Glory of God. The witty ideas that are inside of you were meant to reflect and glorify Christ the King.

Through you mankind will see that there is a God. Through your gifts, talents, skills, and abilities mankind will see that

God exists. Your gifts were meant to point to and glorify Christ the King. Colossians 1:17 KJV declares, "And he is before all things, and by him all things consist." All things exist because of Christ—even your gifts. Surrender your gifts to Christ.

Your gifts weren't meant to stay stagnant. Your gifts weren't meant to fertilize the dead ground of the valley. Your gifts were meant to praise and glorify God. David declares in Psalms 115:17 KJV, "The dead praise not the Lord, neither any that go down into silence." The dead cannot praise God. The spiritually inactive cannot praise God. The spiritually inoperative cannot praise God. The double-minded cannot praise God.

According to Strong's Concordance, the Hebrew word for, "Praise", used in Psalms 115:17 KJV is "Halal" (H1984) which means, "To shine, to shine of God's favor, to flash forth light, boast, to be boastful, to be made praiseworthy, to be commended, be worthy of praise, glory, to make one's boast, to make a fool of, make into a fool."

The gifts, innovation, insight, and wisdom that's inside of you were meant to *Halal* God. God has set you on a hill to *Halal* Him. Your gifts were meant to Halal Christ. Your gifts were meant to shine. Your gifts, skills, talents, and abilities were meant to *Halal* Christ.

Let your life make a boast unto the Lord. Let your obedience *Halal* the Creator. Let your execution *Halal* God. Let your diligence make a boast unto the Lord. Let what's inside of you spring forth and *Halal* Christ. Let what God has placed inside of you *Halal* Him.

Don't let the vision die. Don't let your dreams die. Don't let your gifts die unused. Don't let your destiny die in the wasteland of hopelessness. Don't waste what God has placed in you. Choose to let every aspect of your life *Halal* Christ our Living King.

PRAYER

Father God, in the Name of Jesus, I will not waste the gifts that You've planted inside of me. Father, I refuse to let the gifts that You have given me to die in the wasteland of the valley.

Lord, lead me. Lord, let the gifts that You've given me glorify You. Father, let the talents that You've given me magnify and extol You.

Father, You are the Author of my praise. Father, You are the Author of my *Halal*. Father, You are the Captain of my ship and Architect of my destiny. Lord, lead me and guide my heart.

Father, let Your Light shine through me. I will not let the gifts that You've given me go underutilized. Father, You are the Source of my strength, and in You do I trust. Father, my hope is in You.

In Jesus' Name. Amen.

Day 15

MAN SHALL NOT LIVE BY BREAD ALONE

But he answered and said, It is written, Man shall not live by bread alone, but by every word that proceedeth out of the mouth of God.

MATTHEW 4:4 KJV

While Jesus was in the wilderness, He declared that man shall not live by bread or by natural means alone—but by every Word that proceeds out of the mouth of God. Choose to treasure and eat what God has declared over your life. Meditate and digest what God has declared over your destiny, life, and your family.

According to Strong's Concordance, the Greek word for "Word" is, "Rhema" (G4487) which means, "That which is or has been uttered by the living voice." Let the Living Word of God live within the borders of your heart. Your God-given dreams, vision, ideas, gifts, talents, and abilities are Lively Words spoken over you by God Himself.

God declares in Jeremiah 1:5 KJV, "Before I formed thee in the belly I knew thee; and before thou camest forth out of the womb I sanctified thee, and I ordained thee a prophet unto the nations." Before you were formed—God knew you. Before

God formed you in your mother's womb—God knew you and declared His Living Word over you.

God's Word is alive, and His Word wasn't meant to stay stagnant. His Word wasn't meant to stay still. His Word wasn't meant to sit dormant. His Word is alive and is full of Power and Authority. Let His Word come alive in you.

Hebrews 4:12 AMPC declares, "For the Word that God speaks is alive and full of power [making it active, operative, energizing, and effective]; it is sharper than any two-edged sword, penetrating to the dividing line of the breath of life (soul) and [the immortal] spirit, and of joints and marrow [of the deepest parts of our nature], exposing and sifting and analyzing and judging the very thoughts and purposes of the heart."

Choose to be sustained by the Living, breathing, and active Word of God. Let His Word breathe into your life. Let His Word come alive within your purpose. Your life and light weren't meant to stay hidden. The Word, Wisdom, and Insight that God has poured inside of you is sharper than any weapon of the enemy.

Isaiah 54:17 KJV declares, "No weapon that is formed against thee shall prosper; and every tongue that shall rise against thee in judgment thou shalt condemn. This is the heritage of the servants of the Lord, and their righteousness is of me, saith the Lord." The Amplified Version expounds upon Isaiah 54:17 AMPC in the following manner, "But no weapon that is formed against you shall prosper, and every tongue that shall rise against you in judgment you shall show to be in the wrong. This [peace, righteousness, security, triumph over opposition] is the heritage of the servants of the Lord [those in whom the ideal Servant of the Lord is reproduced]; this is the righteousness or the vindication which they obtain from Me [this is that which I impart to them as their justification], says the Lord."

His Word is your weapon against the snares, tactics, traps, strongholds, power, and strategies of the enemy. Luke 10:19 KJV declares, "Behold, I give unto you power to tread on serpents and scorpions, and over all the power of the enemy: and nothing shall by any means hurt you." When the enemy comes to attack your purpose—choose to use the Word of God to dethrone the enemy in every area of your life. When the enemy comes to stunt your destiny—choose to deploy the Word of God to disarm the power of the enemy in every area of your life.

God's Word is stronger than the power and strength of the enemy. Choose not to live by bread alone—but by the Living and Active Word of God.

PRAYER

Father God, in the Name of Jesus, I choose to live by every Word that proceeds out of Your mouth. Father, I choose to take heed to Your Word. Father, I choose to obey Your Word. Father, I choose to build my life upon Your Word.

Father, Your Word is a lamp unto my feet and a light unto my path. Father, Your Word lights my destiny. Lord, lead me. Father, Your Word is alive and is full of power. Father, Your Word is alive and is full of Authority.

Father, let Your Word come alive within the walls of my heart. Father Your Word is active, operative, energizing, and effective and it is sharper than any two-edged sword.

Father, Your Word is stronger than any weapon of the enemy. Father, Your Word crushes every snare and tactic of the enemy.

In Jesus' Name. Amen.

Day 16

SATAN DESIRES TO SIFT YOU AS WHEAT

And the Lord said, Simon, Simon, behold, Satan hath desired to have you, that he may sift you as wheat

LUKE 22:31 KJV

The enemy desires to sift you as wheat. The enemy desires to sift your gifts, talents, and abilities as wheat. The enemy wants to sift your gifts and let your talents sit inactive, dormant, and inoperative. The enemy wants you to die unfulfilled.

Jesus declares in John 10:10 KJV, "The thief cometh not, but for to steal, and to kill, and to destroy: I am come that they might have life, and that they might have it more abundantly." The thief comes to steal your joy. The thief comes to steal your purpose. The thief comes to kill your destiny. The thief comes to destroy your dreams. Christ came to give you life. Christ came to restore your destiny. Christ came to set you free.

The New International Version expounds on John 10:10 NIV in the following manner, "The thief comes only to steal and kill and destroy; I have come that they may have life, and have it to the full." Live your life to the full. Don't let your dreams, talents, gifts, and abilities rot in the wilderness. You were created to live a full and satisfying life.

You were built to create and innovate. You were created for such a time as this. Don't let your destiny die. Take the next step forward. Launch that dream. Build that business. Write that book. Dreams weren't meant to stay in a dream state. Dreams were meant to be birthed. Let God give life to your dead dreams.

Gifts, dreams, talents, and abilities were meant to feed the world. Dreams weren't meant to stay dormant. Nothing that God declares remains stagnant. Your God-given dreams were designed by God to feed generations.

What God has put inside of you was meant to lead and inspire nations. What God has poured inside of you was meant to enlarge and multiply. When God's Word goes forth—it is alive and will not return unto Him void.

Isaiah 55:11 KJV declares, "So shall my word be that goeth forth out of my mouth: it shall not return unto me void, but it shall accomplish that which I please, and it shall prosper in the thing whereto I sent it." Your purpose will not return unto God void.

The gifts, talents, skills, and abilities that God has placed inside of you—will not return unto God void. The world is waiting on you to deploy the gifts that God has placed inside of you. The world is yearning to digest what God has placed inside of you.

Eyes have not seen, nor have ears heard what God has placed inside of you. Let God unveil what's inside of you. Your gifts were meant to *Halal* Christ. Your gifts were meant to worship and honor Christ the King. Let God show you off to the world. It's time to let your light shine. Choose to light up the world.

PRAYER

Father God, in the Name of Jesus, I cast my crown at Your feet. Every gift, every talent, every skill, every ability I lay them at Your Throne. For You are my Lord and I bow to You.

Father God, in the Name of Jesus, the enemy will not sift the gifts that You have placed inside of me. Father, I choose to surrender my gifts to You.

Father, use my hands to build. Father, use my heart to lead. Father, lead my feet to build Your Kingdom.

Lord, enlarge my territory. Father, give me the strength to launch. Lord, increase my faith. Lord, grant me the courage to pursue everything that You have for me.

In Jesus' Name. Amen.

Day 17

OBEDIENCE BREAKS CYCLES

For since the beginning of the world men have not heard, nor perceived by the ear, neither hath the eye seen, O God, beside thee, what he hath prepared for him that waiteth for him.

ISAIAH 64:4 KJV

Your obedience breaks generational cycles. Your obedience will shift the trajectory of your family's bloodline. Your obedience today could transform your family's lineage forever. One act of obedience could shift the trajectory of your family's legacy forever.

David killed Goliath and his name was written in history forever. Abraham obeyed God and his name was changed—transforming his legacy forever. Esther stepped out in faith and saved an entire nation. Gideon obeyed God and led an entire generation.

Noah obeyed God and saved his family from destruction. Moses obeyed God and delivered millions of people out of bondage. Joshua obeyed God and led a new generation into the Promised Land.

When you obey God, your life will never be the same. What has God given you to accomplish? What God-given vision has God placed in your heart to carry out? What business have you not started, finished, or executed upon?

What's sitting in your heart that's left unwritten? What witty idea has God given you to execute upon? What God-given assignment have you not carried out because of an excuse? Excuses inhibit your destiny. Disobedience restricts you from fulfilling your purpose. You were created and called by God to function and fulfill your purpose. Choose to fulfill the mandate that's on your life. Do what God has told you to do.

Generational cycles of poverty, perversion, addiction, and every other entanglement can be broken through your obedience. Choose to diligently submit to God and execute upon what He commands you to do.

Deuteronomy 28:1 KJV declares, "And it shall come to pass, if thou shalt hearken diligently unto the voice of the Lord thy God, to observe and to do all his commandments which I command thee this day, that the Lord thy God will set thee on high above all nations of the earth:" When you follow God's Word and deploy His strategies, you'll break generational cycles and patterns.

You were created on purpose. You were created by God to fulfill a particular purpose in the Earth. Ephesians 2:10 KJV declares, "For we are his workmanship, created in Christ Jesus unto good works, which God hath before ordained that we should walk in them."

Think about it, you were created by an all-knowing, all-powerful, and omnipresent God. The God who created you, knows everything, exists everywhere at the same time, and holds all power in His Hands—and He decided to create you and place you on Earth at this very moment. God set you on Earth, at this moment in time to accomplish a specific purpose.

Imagine how special you must be to God. God looked across the spectrum of time and created you! He set you on Earth that it might please Him. His creation of you pleases Him. You are His creation. You are His True Delight. You belong to Him. Now is your time. Fulfill and carry out what God has placed in your heart.

God gave you the authority to lead, rule, and to carry out the assignment that He has ordained you to complete. Write that book, build that business, launch that venture, change the world, and feed the heart of nations around the world through what's inside of you. Write that song, lead that organization, and build what God has poured inside of you.

What has God poured inside of you? What assignment(s) has God given you to complete? What gift(s) has God given you to share with the world? The gifts that God has placed inside of you—eyes have not seen nor have ears heard of the wisdom that God has placed inside of you.

Release that gift and pour out what God has placed inside of you to the world. Choose to obey God. Families are waiting. Nations are waiting. Generations are hungry for what God has planted inside of you. It's time to feed the nations. Choose to obey God. The world is waiting.

PRAYER

Father God, in the Name of Jesus, I will release the gifts, talents, and abilities that You've placed inside of me.

Father, I will pour out what You have poured into me. I will lead, build, and launch what You have commanded me to build.

Father, I am Your Workmanship. Father, I was intentionally crafted to glorify You. Father, I choose to glorify You. Father, I choose to obey You. Father, I choose to *Halal* You.

Lord, use my hands to do what You've called me to do. Father, my heart surrenders to You. Father, give me the strength to execute. Lord, enlarge my territory and shift the trajectory of my destiny.

In Jesus' Name. Amen.

Day 18

FOR I KNOW THE THOUGHTS

For I know the thoughts that I think toward you, saith the Lord, thoughts of peace, and not of evil, to give you an expected end.

JEREMIAH 29:11 KJV

God created you with a specific purpose in mind. You are His creation, and you are not a mistake. You were not placed and planted on Earth by accident. You were intentionally created by God Himself. You were born for such a time as this.

The gifts, talents, strengths, and abilities that God has invested inside of you were deposited on purpose. Your gifts have purpose. Your talents have meaning. Your skills, strengths, and abilities all have purpose. God knows His thoughts towards you. Your journey has purpose. He has plans for your success and not your failure.

The Amplified Version expounds on Jeremiah 29:11 AMPC in the following manner, "For I know the thoughts and plans that I have for you, says the Lord, thoughts and plans for welfare and peace and not for evil, to give you hope in your final outcome." God knows your final outcome. God wouldn't give you an assignment that you didn't have the capacity to finish.

God expects you to finish. God expects you to expand. God expects you to grow. God expects you to enlarge. God does not want you to stay stuck and stagnant. God personally crafted the Blueprint that He has for you.

The New Living Translation expounds upon Jeremiah 29:11 NLT in the following manner, "For I know the plans I have for you," God desires to give you a future and an expected end. God desires to give you hope. Don't let your dreams die in the place where your hope died. Don't let your vision die in the place of your last failure. Choose to let the guilt, shame, and defeat of the past go.

Don't let the fear of your last failure keep you enslaved to its sting. Don't let the fear of your last attempt keep you enslaved to its bondage. Keep moving forward. Keep moving towards what God has commanded you to do.

Don't confuse your small beginnings with your final outcome. Just because you've had a small start does not mean that your end will be small. Your small beginning is only the starting point. Don't let small beginnings discourage you from moving forward.

Don't let your small beginnings limit your vision. Don't let your small beginnings hold you back from pursuing everything that God has for you. Learn from the mistakes of the past and take the next step forward. Don't stay stuck in the mistakes and mediocrity of the past. Decide to move forward. It's time to go. It's time to launch.

God wants you to succeed. He wants you to excel. God knows His plans towards you. He's already planned your success. He's planned for you to be successful. Choose to trust God. Your success is in His Hands.

PRAYER

Father God, in the Name of Jesus, I choose to launch with You. Father, I choose to learn from the mistakes of the past and continue to move forward in You.

Father, I choose not to stay stuck in the mediocrity of the past. Father, I choose to move forward. Father, I choose to keep moving towards what You have commanded me to do.

Father, I refuse to let small beginnings discourage me from fulfilling purpose and moving forward in my destiny. Father, I will not allow small beginnings to limit the vision that You have poured into me.

Father, I refuse to let the mistakes of the past paralyze my next step. Father, I repent and turn to You. Father, I refuse to stay stuck in the mediocrity of the past and I choose to serve You.

In Jesus' Name. Amen.

Day 19

IT'S TIME TO LAUNCH

Now when he had left speaking, he said unto Simon, Launch out into the deep, and let down your nets for a draught. And Simon answering said unto him, Master, we have toiled all the night, and have taken nothing: nevertheless at thy word I will let down the net. And when they had this done, they inclosed a great multitude of fishes: and their net brake.

LUKE 5:4-6 KJV

Launch out into the deep. Launch into the unknown. God is with you. He's waiting on you in the deep. He's waiting on you to respond to His Word. He's waiting on you to take the next step. Take the first step and obey God. Choose to follow His Instruction. It's time to launch. It's time to go into the deep.

Because of Peter's obedience—his name was written forever in the hearts of generations that read about this moment found in Luke 5:4-6 KJV. Because Peter obeyed God—his nets broke. Let God break your nets. Let your obedience bring forth an abundant harvest so large that your boat begins to sink. Let your obedience shift the lives of families. Let your obedience shift the trajectory of future generations.

Notice what Luke 5:6 KJV declares, "...And when they had this done, they inclosed a great multitude of fishes: and their net brake." It was only after Peter obeyed Christ that the miraculous net-breaking harvest came forth. Obedience is the prerequisite for breakthrough.

Notice what Luke 5:6 KJV declares, "...they inclosed a great multitude of fishes..." Interestingly enough, not only did Peter and his team catch many fish, but the Bible denotes that they caught "fishes," which indicates multiple types of fish. Their net could not contain the harvest that was coming. Their net could not hold the quantity and quality of fish that came because of their obedience.

Think about it, what if Peter had not obeyed Christ? What if Peter had stopped after his last failed attempt? What if Peter chose to settle with the results that he previously had the night before? Peter had declared that he had toiled all night and he had caught nothing.

Peter was an experienced fisherman—and yet he caught nothing. Peter, and his team, tried to catch fish all throughout the night—yet they had no success. Peter expended his time, his energy, and his resources in an effort to catch fish—but to no avail, he had no success.

It wasn't until Jesus spoke the following words to Peter, "Launch into the deep..." when Peter's season shifted from toiling to flourishing. It wasn't until Peter obeyed Christ and executed once more. Even though Peter toiled in the last season—Peter decided to trust God again. It's time to trust God again. It's time to launch. It's time to launch into the deep and let down your nets for a catch.

Maybe, you're toiling in the wrong place. Maybe, you're toiling in shallow waters. Maybe, you're letting down your net in the wrong place. Maybe, you're trying to do it on your own. Don't do it alone. Don't do it without Christ. Don't build it without Christ. Whatever your "it" may be—don't go fishing without Christ. Don't cast your nets without Christ. It's time to launch into the deep.

PRAYER

Father God, in the Name of Jesus, I choose to follow You. Father, I will obey Your Voice. Father, I will obey Your Word. Father, I will not cast my nets before Your Timing.

Father, I choose to follow You into the deep. Father, I will launch when You tell me to launch. Lord, I will follow You. Father, I will launch with You. Father, like Peter, I choose to obey Your Voice. Father, at thy Word, I will let down my nets.

Father, equip my hands to do what You've called me to do. Lord, lead me. Lord, direct me. Father, strengthen my nets to do this great work.

In Jesus' Name. Amen.

Day 20

TOILED ALL NIGHT

And Simon answering said unto him, Master, we have toiled all the night, and have taken nothing: nevertheless at thy word I will let down the net.

LUKE 5:5 KJV

Notice, in Luke 5:5 KJV, Peter was a skilled and experienced fisherman and yet he toiled all night. Don't let your experience, gifts, talents, abilities, and intellect block you from executing in God's timing. Notice the keyword used in Luke 5:5 KJV, "Nevertheless". "Master, we have toiled all the night, and have taken nothing: nevertheless at thy word I will let down the net."

Even though Peter was experienced, he abandoned his logical way of thinking. Even though Peter was skilled, he decided to follow the instruction of Christ. Peter decided to put his previous experience behind him, and decided to launch based upon God's Word.

Instead of launching based upon his own skill, intellect, and expertise—this time Peter launched with Christ. This time Peter launched when God told him to launch.

Peter obeyed Christ and reaped unprecedented success. Peter and his team were not prepared for the harvest that God had prepared for them. There was a harvest waiting for Peter out in the deep.

What if Peter had not listened to the instructions of Christ to go out into the deep? What if Peter had stayed on the shore? What if Peter had not obeyed God? What if Peter stayed stagnant and focused on his last failed attempt? What if Peter never went fishing with Christ?

One Word from God could change your life—forever. One Word from God could shift and transform your destiny. What if Peter had never launched out into the deep? What if you refuse to launch out into the deep? Generations are waiting on your obedience. Generations are waiting on your "nevertheless."

Thousands of years later, Peter's obedience shaped the hearts of generations who've read about this moment with Christ. One moment of obedience could feed the faith of generations to come. Because of Peter's "nevertheless" we now have the benefit of reaping from his obedience.

As I pen these words, we're sitting in a moment in time that's more than two-thousand years after this net-breaking experience with Christ. Because of Peter's obedience, this moment has been written on the hearts of many generations. Peter's obedience fueled the faith of many generations. Peter's obedience is penned upon the walls of our hearts even to this day.

What if Peter stayed stagnant and never said, "nevertheless?" Because of Peter's "yes" we have the benefit of launching into the deep. Generations are able to launch into the deep when you say yes to your call. Generations are able to go farther and deeper because of your "yes."

Through Peter's "nevertheless" Peter caught more than fish—thousands of years later Peter captured our hearts. Because of Peter's obedience, our faith is stretched and strengthened. On the other side of your "yes"—nations are waiting. Because of your "yes"—you will write upon the hearts of those that come after you.

Choose to submit your nets to Christ and write upon the hearts of future generations. Let Christ remove the "Heart Scales" of the past. Let the past go. Don't let the toiling of the past harden your heart. Don't let the toiling of the past block you from saying "nevertheless."

Let God write upon your heart and choose to launch out into the deep. It's time to try again. It's time to build again. It's time to write again. It's time to lead again. It's time to sing again. It's time to fish again. It's time to launch out into the deep with Christ.

PRAYER

Father God, in the Name of Jesus, I choose to launch with You. Father, I will not let my talent, skills, gifts, and abilities block me from listening to You. Father, I will follow Your Voice. Father, I will follow Your Word. Father, I choose to launch again.

Father, I choose to abandon my logical way of thinking and I choose to follow You. Father, I choose to put behind my previous experience and with my whole heart, I will follow You. Father, You are my Lord and I fully surrender to You. Lord, I bow to You.

Father, I surrender to Your Way of doing things. Father, remove the "Heart Scales" that block me from launching into the deep. Father, heal my heart from past failed attempts.

Father, I refuse to let the toiling of the past harden my heart. Father, I refuse to let the toiling of the last season block me from pursuing You with my whole heart.

Father, I will not let my last failure block me from launching out into the deep. Father, I will cast my nets again with You. In Jesus' Name. Amen.

Day 21

BE STRONG AND COURAGEOUS

> *This is my command—be strong and courageous! Do not be afraid or discouraged. For the Lord your God is with you wherever you go.*
>
> JOSHUA 1:9 NLT

Be strong and courageous. God is with you wherever you go. May Christ write upon the walls of your heart. May Christ write upon the "Heart Path" of your destiny.

May Christ lead you to triumphantly conquer new territories. May Christ order your steps. May He write upon the walls of your destiny. May God give you the strength to fight again.

May God give you the courage to try again. May God give you the courage to write again. May God give you the strength to build again. May God give you the courage to lead again.

May God rewrite your story. May He give you His Peace that surpasses all understanding. May He encourage you in your darkest hour. May He shine His Light upon every area of your heart.

May He give you the strength to pursue the Promise that He's set before you. May He satisfy you all the days of your life. May your cup overflow with blessings. May He give you peace on every side. May He give you rest on every side. May He establish you. May He establish your borders.

May He make your feet like hinds' feet and cause you to walk upon high places. May He cause the work of your hands to flourish. May He cause everything that your hands touch to prosper.

May He reset you. May He rewrite your story. May He enlarge you. May He keep you. May He protect you.

May He make your enemies your footstool. May He break every generational curse and cycle. May He lead you beside still waters. May He restore your soul.

May He bless your coming in and your going out. May He bless the work of your hands. May He bless your thoughts and ideas. May He increase you more and more.

May He bless your witty ideas, inventions, processes, and strategies. May He give you the strength, power, tenacity, and fortitude to get wealth.

May He bless the fruit of your womb. May your seed be blessed. May your house be blessed. May everything that you touch be blessed. May everything that comes out of you be blessed.

May He be with you wherever you go. May you meditate and dwell upon His Word day and night. May His Word fall not to the wayside. May God bless you from the north, south, east, and west. May opportunities overtake you. May His blessings consume you.

May you deal wisely in everything that you do. May you remember the Lord your God—for it is He who has given you the power to get wealth. May you hide His Word deep within the bedrock of your heart. May you follow, keep, and obey His Word day and night.

May He be your Strong Tower. May you run to Him. May you conquer every fear. May you tread upon serpents and scorpions. May your enemies who come to eat up your flesh—stumble and fall. May those who rise up against you flee seven ways. May the Lord God shine His Light upon your life forevermore.

May He write a new song upon your heart. May He write new lyrics upon the borders of your heart. May He lead you. May He guide you. May He give you the strength to fight again. May He give you the strength to pick up the pen again. May your pen be your sword to write upon the hearts of generations.

May He give you the strength to start again. May He give you the faith to take your next step. May He give you the strength to finish the good work that He's placed inside of you. May He direct your footsteps. May He walk with you. May He continually lead your path.

May He breathe upon the work of your hands. May He guide you into uncharted territory. May He break every habit, cycle, yoke, and bondage. May He remove the yoke of the wilderness. May He remove the bitter stain of the past. May He remove the bitter stain of your last failed attempt.

May He bless your days. May everything that your hands touch flourish and become fruitful and multiply. May He write upon the heart of your destiny. May He satisfy you. May He lead you. May He comfort you.

May you go in and possess every Promise that God has for you. May you be blessed. May your seed be blessed. May your seed's seed be blessed. May you go in peace and possess the land.

In Jesus' Name. Amen.

FOR MORE BOOKS VISIT
www.VanceKJackson.com

www.ingramcontent.com/pod-product-compliance
Lightning Source LLC
Chambersburg PA
CBHW030914080526
44589CB00010B/294